What Do We Know About
the Nazca Lines?

by Ben Hubbard

illustrated by Dede Putra

Penguin Workshop

For Malc, Smit, and Tom: FM—BH

PENGUIN WORKSHOP
An imprint of Penguin Random House LLC, New York

First published in the United States of America by Penguin Workshop,
an imprint of Penguin Random House LLC, New York, 2024

Visit us online at penguinrandomhouse.com.

Library of Congress Cataloging-in-Publication Data is available.

Printed in the United States of America

ISBN 9780593662533 (paperback)   10 9 8 7 6 5 4 3 2 1 WOR
ISBN 9780593662540 (library binding)   10 9 8 7 6 5 4 3 2 1 WOR

Contents

The pampa

What Do We Know About the Nazca Lines?

One day in 1926, Toribio Mejía Xesspe (say: ZESS-pay) took a hike in the hills near the town of Nazca in southern Peru. From the top of a hill, Mejía Xesspe gazed across the landscape below him, called the Nazca Pampa: a flat, featureless desert plateau around eighty-five square miles in size. Little grows on this barren land, littered with pebbles and rocks.

The pampa is situated high up, around 1,500 feet above sea level. To the east lie the mighty Andes Mountains, and to the west, the Pacific Ocean. On the southern edge of the pampa is the Nazca River; to the north, the Ingenio River. The rivers bring some water to the valleys below them, but little water ever reaches the elevated pampa. In fact, it is one of the driest places on Earth. This is because the Andes Mountains block the clouds that carry water toward the coast. As a result, less than one millimeter of rain falls on the pampa each year.

To Mejía Xesspe, who was an archaeologist (a person who analyzes artifacts to study human history), the pampa seemed like a giant wasteland. But when he looked more carefully, he could see something strange crisscrossing the surface of the flat land below him. It looked like lines. Some of the lines crossed others; some stretched

hundreds of feet into the distance. Some seemed to form shapes, such as triangles and rectangles. Others were harder to make out. The pampa looked a bit like a geometry

Toribio Mejía Xesspe

teacher's chalkboard after a busy week of lessons.

Intrigued, Mejía Xesspe walked down to the pampa to take a closer look. Here, he found the lines were more like etchings on the land's surface. The dark desert pebbles had been moved away to reveal the pale sand beneath.

Some of the lines were less than thirty inches wide, but others were as wide as six feet. Their straight edges were too precise to have been made by the flow of water. There were no rivers on the pampa anyway. But this also meant there had been nothing to wash the lines away. They were probably very old.

Finding the lines had surprised Mejía Xesspe. He felt certain that they had been made by people. But he didn't make a big deal about them. At the time, he was making other important discoveries with Julio C. Tello, a famous archaeologist often called the Father of Peruvian Archaeology.

Nazca Lines

To this day, no one has been able to solve the ancient mystery of what became known as the Nazca Lines.

CHAPTER 1
Patterns on the Pampa

Located on the west coast of South America, the country of Peru has a variety of landscapes that include mountains, deserts, beaches, and rain forests. It is comprised of coastal plains in the west, high rugged mountains in the center, and lowland jungle in the east. The Amazon Rain Forest—the largest in South America—covers more than half of Peru. Stretching from north to south are the Andes Mountains. The Andes are so high (averaging between 13,000 and 22,000 feet above sea level) that they can be seen from Peru's Pacific Coast beaches, fifty miles to the west. Peru's west coast is made up of a narrow strip of desert around 1,555 miles long. It is here that ancient cultures such as the

Paracas and Nazca used to live. Later, the Inca Empire took over and built large cities and temples.

The Paracas people were an ancient Peruvian culture who lived between 750 BCE and 200 CE. They existed before the Nazca, but inhabited parts of the same area in Peru's south. They were also a big influence on the Nazca people. Both cultures were famous for their ceramics (pottery), textiles (fabric), and for the way they buried their dead. This included placing the bodies in a crouching position and wrapping them in layers of cloth. Known as "mummy bundles," the bodies were then buried together in an underground chamber.

We know about the Paracas because of Toribio Mejía Xesspe and Julio Tello, who investigated the remains of the culture in the 1920s. In 1929, Tello unearthed a large burial site that contained 429 mummy bundles. This amazing find included ceramics, textiles, and jewels, which helped them to understand the Paracas culture.

Paracas cloth

The Inca

The Inca were a famous South American civilization who built their capital, Cuzco, in what is now Peru. Between the thirteenth and fifteenth centuries, the Inca conquered a vast tract of land that extended from present-day Ecuador to Chile. To control this empire, the Inca kings built

a vast network of roads, fortifications, cities, and temples. Their twelve million subjects worshipped the Inca gods, such as the rain god, Apu Illapu. However, just as the Inca Empire reached its peak in 1532, it was overthrown by conquistadors (conquerors) from Spain. Afterward, whole Inca cities were abandoned and forgotten.

The Inca site of Winay Wayna

Like the Nazca, the Paracas did not have a written language. This means that everything we know about them comes from the objects they left behind. While archaeologists carefully preserve their finds for study, there are people who are simply interested in selling ancient objects to make a profit.

Julio C. Tello

Tello and Mejía Xesspe's important finds at Paracas may explain why Mejía Xesspe did not fully investigate the lines on the Nazca Pampa. However, Mejía Xesspe did talk about the Nazca Lines in a 1939 conference in Lima, Peru's capital. Here, he explained that he thought they were "religious roads," which may have been used for processions. He also wrote a paper about them, although he did not study them further himself. Neither Mejía Xesspe's talk nor his paper seemed to generate much interest.

One person who may have attended Mejía Xesspe's talk, however, was American historian Paul Kosok. At that time, Kosok was in Lima, studying ancient cultures. In 1941, Kosok traveled to the Nazca Pampa to look at the lines himself. They immediately grabbed his attention. Kosok and his wife,

Paul Kosok

Rose, then moved to Nazca to study them further. Their work marked a turning point in learning why the Nazca Lines may have been made.

The Kosoks found that actually making the lines had been quite simple. It involved moving the darker stones and pebbles to the sides while creating a shallow trench in the lighter sand underneath. The stones and pebbles then formed a border on either side of the trench. These borders ranged in size from one inch to three feet high. Other stones were removed and placed in piles.

Tomb Robbers

Tomb robbers, or looters, have been stealing objects left by the Nazca for many centuries. These include Nazca ceramics, which collectors have always found desirable. Even today, looters visit sites recently uncovered by archaeologists to see if there are any ancient items worth stealing. These rare and valuable finds are then illegally sold or traded. During their raids on ancient Nazca sites, careless tomb robbers have left objects they did not want strewn across the pampa, including Nazca textiles and bones from burial chambers. Bones and skulls can still be seen on the desert surface today, bleached bright white by the sunlight.

The Kosoks believed that the straight lines were made using simple surveying tools, probably wooden stakes and string, to provide a guide for carving them. Not all the lines were straight: some had curves, spirals, and zigzag shapes. No one is exactly sure how this was done.

The color difference between the light sand of the dug-out line and the darker rocks covering the rest of the pampa made it stand out. From nearby hills, people would have been able to see parts of these images. However, the Kosoks found some of the designs to be massive. Some were hundreds of feet across! This puzzled the couple. There would be no way of seeing these entire images from the hill. The only way to properly view it was from high above it, in the air.

For the Kosoks, this raised an important question. It is one that has confused and divided archaeologists ever since.

935 FEET

The pelican geoglyph, 935 feet long

In 1941, airplanes were still a relatively new invention. The Wright brothers made the first powered flight in 1903, but jet airplanes did not come into use until 1939. Interestingly, some planes flying over the Nazca Pampa had reported seeing lines on the ground even before the Kosoks arrived. But the Nazca themselves did not have planes, of course. So why then had the Nazca made patterns they would never be able to see?

To explore this mystery, the Kosoks hired a plane and took to the air. Even from this height, they found the lines difficult to see clearly. Over the centuries, they had become faint. This was because wind had blown small stones across some of them and covered the paler ground underneath. To make out particular shapes, the Kosoks took aerial photos from the plane and then walked along the ground taking exact measurements.

As they walked, the Kosoks realized that most of the designs ran in a continuous line. They could start in one place, walk around the entire outline of an image, and end up in the same place again. Were these pathways made to walk around? The Kosoks also often found broken pieces of pottery by the sides of the lines. The Nazca were famous for their ceramics, but why were pieces left here? Had the pottery been abandoned by the Nazca or by looters?

Then the Kosoks discovered something even more startling. One set of lines was not in a shape or a pattern, but a picture. It had been created in

the shape of a bird. This was the first geoglyph to be discovered. But it would not be the last.

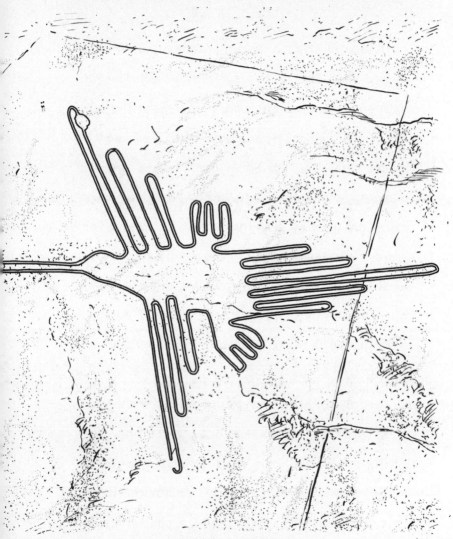

The hummingbird geoglyph

What Are Geoglyphs?

A geoglyph is a design, pattern, or image etched into the earth's surface, usually larger than six feet long and visible only from the air. The word comes from combining *geo*, which means "relating to the earth," and *glyph*, meaning a character or symbol. Geoglyphs are often created by digging into the ground, or removing stones and soil to show a different color underneath. Other geoglyphs are formed from piles of stones or rocks shaped into a design. Most geoglyphs were created long ago by ancient people.

Geoglyphs have been found around the world, from Australia, to the Americas, to Europe. The Uffington White Horse is a famous geoglyph, made in the late Bronze or early Iron Age (between 1740 and 210 BCE), carved into a chalk hillside in Oxfordshire, England. The Nazca Lines, as they came to be known, are perhaps the world's best-known geoglyphs.

The Uffington White Horse

CHAPTER 2
Who Were the Nazca?

The Nazca civilization emerged around 200 BCE, and their influence quickly spread far and wide across southern Peru. At their peak, the Nazca inhabited a region that covered the Ica Valley and the Rio Grande de Nasca drainage, an area of around 4,150 square miles with nine rivers running through it. The Nazca Pampa, where most of the Nazca Lines lie, sits between the Nazca and Ingenio Rivers. Here, next to the rivers, lay fertile valleys where the Nazca grew their crops. The Nazca believed that their gods controlled all natural processes on Earth, including the weather. They would therefore perform ceremonies when they planted crops, hoping the gods would provide them with water for a good harvest.

One of the Nazca gods

Although the Nazca lived across a large area, they were probably not united under one leader. Instead, they mainly lived in small settlements and villages, which were probably controlled by local chiefs. On higher ground, Nazca homes were built on stone terraces and carved into the slopes of hills. On the lower plains, homes were made from wooden posts and woven mats covered in clay plaster. It is possible that Nazca people also inhabited a small city called Ventilla that was situated by the Ingenio River.

The remains of many mud brick houses built into terraces have been discovered there. While some archaeologists believe this to be a Nazca city, others say there is no proof the Nazca lived in large urban centers. Instead, it may have been a religious center.

One such center was called Cahuachi. It was built on the south bank of the Nazca River facing

the pampa on more than seventy acres of land. Cahuachi featured temples, plazas, and a grand pyramid that was once around seventy-five feet high. These large structures were made from mud bricks and covered in a whitewash made with gypsum or lime. It is thought that Cahuachi was used as a large ceremonial center where the Nazca performed rituals and made offerings to their gods.

Cahuachi

Some of these offerings have been uncovered in recent times. They include the sacrificed remains of llamas and guinea pigs, alongside panpipes, feathers, shells, and pieces of pottery. Some offerings were buried in underground chambers. Human heads, probably taken in battle as trophies, were also discovered.

These trophy heads were an important part of Nazca culture. The removal of the heads of Nazca enemies was linked to improving crop harvests.

A Nazca statue of a man holding a trophy head

Sometimes the heads were shown on Nazca pottery with plants growing from their mouths.

During Nazca ceremonies, people wore masks, costumes, and headdresses, and played music and danced. Many ceremonies were held in Cahuachi's large plaza, where the smashing of panpipes and pottery took place. While not in use, the Nazca costumes were kept in storage rooms in Cahuachi. These costumes were made to look like the gods and supernatural beings worshipped by the Nazca, such as the Mythical Spotted Cat and the Mythical Killer Whale.

Nazca panpipes

Many textiles created by the Nazca have been excavated from Cahuachi. Made of llama, vicuña, and alpaca wool, and often cotton, some of these have been found completely intact. One ceremonial cloak, two feet by five feet and made of cotton and wool, includes yellow, red, and green colors. These colors came from insect, animal, and vegetable pigments. (Pigments are substances that give plants and animals their color. These can be extracted to make paint and dye.)

Ceremonial cloak

Attached to the cloak are small, three-dimensional figures, also made from wool, depicting people walking in procession. There are ninety figures in this procession, each of them different. It is possible that they represent real people. They are shown in costume and carrying panpipes, flutes, and fans.

Figures in procession

When not performing ceremonies, the Nazca dressed in less elaborate clothes. Nazca women wore long tunics, with an ankle-length wrap over the top. They grew their hair long and sometimes added headdresses. Men, too, wore tunics with slits for the head and arms and loincloths underneath. Nazca tunics were made with colors such as blue, gold, gray, green, pink, and red. Men wore a range of headgear depending on their occupation. Nazca men were usually farmers, animal herders, fishermen, warriors, or shamans (a type of priest). Farmers wore cone-shaped hats, while others wore headbands with tassels, fox fur, or bird feathers. Some men had necklaces made of shell, while both men and women wore square earrings cut from shells. It is thought that Nazca people often went barefoot, although some sandals have been recovered.

In addition to their amazing woven creations, the Nazca were famous for their ceramics. Much of what we know about the Nazca comes from their pottery. Before the Nazca, the Paracas people fired (baked) their pots in a kiln (a very hot oven) and then painted the hardened surface. The Nazca perfected a form of ceramic making that involved painting their pots with colors before firing them in a kiln.

Using this method, the Nazca made countless pots, double-spouted bottles, panpipes, trumpets, and models of creatures, such as lobsters and fish. Scenes showing Nazca people, their gods, and their ceremonies were also painted on large pots, bowls, and plates. At other times, the pots were decorated with lines and patterns: spirals, zigzags, wavy lines, triangles, and diamonds. There are also hummingbirds, monkeys, and spiders.

Perhaps unsurprisingly, these are the images that began to be found more and more in the 1940s, etched into the Nazca Pampa just north of Cahuachi.

CHAPTER 3
Ancient Astronomy

Paul and Rose Kosok continued studying the Nazca Lines throughout 1941. Their aim was to discover why the lines had been created there. Then, on the evening of June 22, they thought they had found their answer. While sitting near the bird geoglyph, the couple noticed the sun was setting exactly over the end of one of the lines. They also remembered it was the shortest day of the year in the Southern Hemisphere (the area of Earth that is south of the equator). "With a great thrill we realized at once we had apparently discovered the key to the riddle," Paul Kosok wrote. The Kosoks' theory was that the Nazca had made the line to mark the winter solstice (the shortest day of the year).

The theory seemed to fit. It would explain
why the Nazca had made images so large that
they couldn't be seen from ground level. Could

they have been simply making a giant calendar to record events such the longest and shortest days of the year? The Kosoks believed that the pampa lines might make up "the largest astronomy book in the world."

Paul Kosok was so enthusiastic about his theory that he hired a young German mathematician to help him investigate further. Maria Reiche (say: RIE-sha) had been living in Peru since 1932. She went to the Nazca Pampa in late 1941 and immediately became fascinated by the lines. She observed the lines from the ground on December 22, the longest day of the year in the Southern Hemisphere. She thought that the shapes and lines did indeed line up with the setting sun. Reiche agreed with the Kosoks' theory connecting the lines

Maria Reiche

to movements of the sun and possibly other stars and planets in the sky.

In 1948, Reiche moved to southern Peru so she could study the Nazca Lines in earnest. She devoted the rest of her life to this pursuit, working at it for more than fifty years. Living in an adobe hut near the pampa, Reiche drew diagrams of the lines on paper and then toilet paper when she ran out. She had to hang her drawings from a clothesline so mice would not eat them.

Decades later, Reiche moved to a local hotel and gave tours of the lines. She became known as "The Lady of the Lines."

Reiche dedicated herself not only to studying the lines but also to preserving and restoring them. To restore the lines, Reiche swept away the tiny dark stones that had blown across them. She drew detailed pictures of each one. She convinced the Peruvian Air Force to take aerial photos of the Nazca Lines. The restored lines could now be seen far more clearly than when the Kosoks had flown above them a few years earlier. This also helped Reiche identify what the lines looked like. She made some amazing discoveries.

Reiche found that the bird discovered by the Kosoks was not the only picture geoglyph on the pampa. In fact, there were more than two dozen! The first one Reiche saw was a giant spider, 150 feet long. Then she found a monkey,

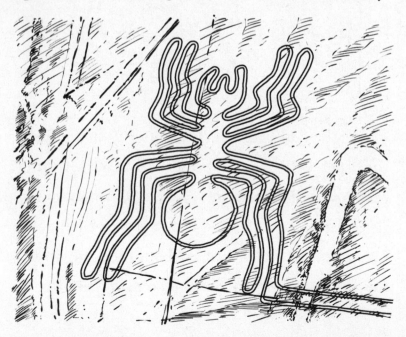

a dog, a condor, a pelican, a lizard, a fox, a killer whale, and a plant. There were some weird creature mixtures: One seemed to be half-insect half-bird, and another half-cat half-fish.

There were a total of eighteen bird geoglyphs. Some of these depicted hummingbirds, one of which was 300 feet long, with a 150-foot beak.

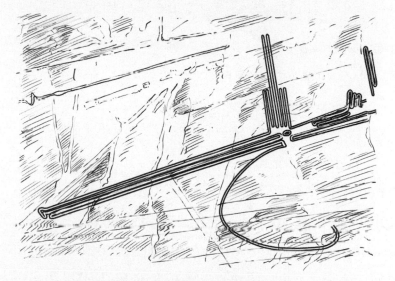

Frigatebird geoglyph

Another bird geoglyph had a beak made from a long zigzagging line. There was an enormous frigatebird (a type of seabird), measuring 600 feet from wingtip to wingtip.

Frigatebird

Reiche found that each of the animal geoglyphs was made in one single, continuous line. It reminded her of a child's drawing game, where a player has to complete a picture without lifting the pen off the paper. Reiche believed this meant that the picture geoglyphs were ceremonial pathways. They had no beginning and no end point. A procession of people could walk around the outline of a particular animal through its twists and turns and then exit at the same place they started from.

There were still confusing aspects to the lines, however. Did the animal geoglyphs point toward astronomical bodies in the sky, for example? And why did many of the straight lines and geometric shapes cross over the picture geoglyphs?

Reiche thought she had the answer. She believed that many of the straight lines made up a calendar, while the picture geoglyphs showed specific groups of stars, called constellations. Reiche said the monkey geoglyph, for example, was the same constellation we know as Ursa Major, or the Great Bear.

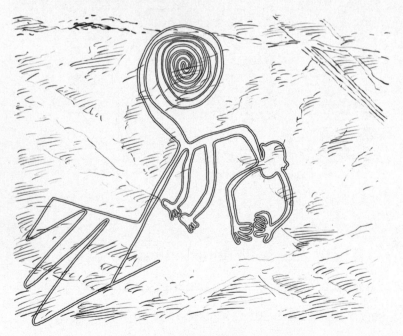

Monkey geoglyph

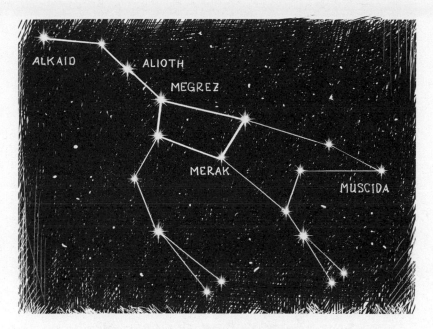

Ursa Major in the night sky

For decades, Reiche's and the Kosoks' theories were generally accepted as having revealed the truth about the Nazca Lines. Maria Reiche became something of a Nazca Lines celebrity, and her work attracted attention from scientists and nonscientists alike. This led to new theories about the Nazca Lines that captured the imagination of many people around the world.

Ancient Star Studies

People have been fascinated by patterns of stars for thousands of years. Early humans noticed that certain star clusters were grouped in shapes of animals, or people. By the second century CE, the Greeks had named their constellations, such as Ursa Major (the Great Bear) and Orion (the Hunter).

Some ancient cultures also built structures to mark the movement of the sun. The structures would then function as calendars to help people chart the seasons. This allowed them to plan different aspects of their lives, including when to plant their crops. Stonehenge in England, a circle of standing stones, is thought to be one such structure. In Mexico, the ancient Maya people built observatories to track the movement of the stars. By the first century BCE, they had created a calendar that was more accurate than European calendars of that time.

Maya calendar

CHAPTER 4
Aliens and Hot Air

In the 1960s, some strange new theories emerged about why the Nazca Lines existed.

The most famous of these was by Swiss author Erich von Däniken. In his 1968 book *Chariots of the Gods?*, von Däniken wrote that many ancient cultures had been influenced by extraterrestrials who had arrived on Earth from space. He thought these cultures could have included the ancient Egyptians, the ancient Britons, and the indigenous people of Easter Island. Von Däniken said extraterrestrials taught the ancient Egyptians how to build pyramids, and that they also visited the Nazca people and created the first lines.

According to von Däniken, the alien beings might have used the Nazca Pampa as an airfield, a place to land their spaceships. He suggested that the Nazca made the large tracks in the desert to identify a place for the aliens to land. Could these tracks be the lines we see today?

Erich von Däniken

Perhaps the Nazca assumed they had been visited by the gods. The spaceships were fiery chariots of the sky gods, according to von Däniken. In a sequel to *Chariots of the Gods?*, and in later writings, von Däniken expanded his theory, claiming that after the extraterrestrials had gone, the Nazca maintained and extended the lines they left behind. They also created picture geoglyphs, such as the birds, that look like spaceships. They then performed ceremonies inside these geoglyphs, hoping the sky gods would come back. Von Däniken said that one of the geoglyphs, known today as "the astronaut" (also known as the "owl man"), is an image of the alien beings.

Astronaut geoglyph

Von Däniken also believed that there were many images of extraterrestrials on Nazca pottery. Later, some skulls were even discovered at Nazca sites. They were elongated and "not of earthly origin," von Däniken claimed. However, after it was proved that the skulls were human, von Däniken changed his mind. He said they must have been elongated (purposely lengthened) to look like the visiting spacemen.

Eric von Däniken's theories were controversial, but also hugely popular. *Chariots of the Gods?* went on to sell more than seven million copies worldwide. Television documentaries were made about his theories on extraterrestrials and von Däniken himself became a sought-after public speaker. The idea that alien beings had visited the people of Earth in ancient times sparked the public's imagination. Many people wanted to believe that alien beings had visited Earth because that might explain so many ancient mysteries.

Elongated Skulls

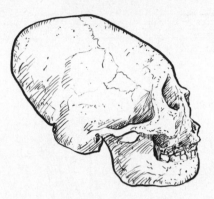

The Nazca believed that an elongated—higher and more cone-shaped—skull was a sign of beauty. They distorted the skulls of babies to give them a different shape than the natural skulls they were born with. To do this, they tied a cushion across the front of a baby's head and a wooden board across the back. This would make the skull grow to a taller shape instead of a round one.

This was a common practice, but not all Nazca skulls were reshaped in this way. In a 1988 sample of 102 skulls from a Nazca burial site, only 68 percent had been manipulated to be elongated. Many other ancient cultures around the world practiced similar skull shaping. These included the Alans people of Iran, the Maya, the Inca, and some indigenous North American nations, including the Choctaw and the Chehalis.

Soon everyone seemed to know about the Nazca Lines. Tourists began flocking to Peru to see these "alien lines."

Von Däniken's book enraged Maria Reiche, who said his ideas were absurd. Scholars and scientists were also horrified by von Däniken's theories. His book was quickly found to have countless inaccuracies. Even his descriptions of the lines themselves did not match reality. The famous American scientist Carl Sagan wrote: "I know of no recent books so riddled with logical and factual errors as the works of von Däniken."

Carl Sagan

Von Däniken himself insisted his ideas were true.

After von Däniken's book, there were no

further claims about alien visitors creating the Nazca Lines. However, there was a new theory about the Nazca creating the lines from the sky. In the 1970s, American explorer Jim Woodman said that he believed the Nazca people had invented an early form of hot air balloon. Made of cotton and reeds, the Nazca hot air balloons could have

Jim Woodman

been used to both make the lines and view them. Woodman also suspected that the Nazca sent their dead off in these balloons. An engineer told him that the balloons could have floated west and crash-landed somewhere over the Pacific Ocean.

To prove his theory, Woodman built a hot air balloon using only local materials. He even made it fly for fourteen minutes. However, although Woodman had been to see the Nazca Lines and studied their textiles, he was mistaken in his theory.

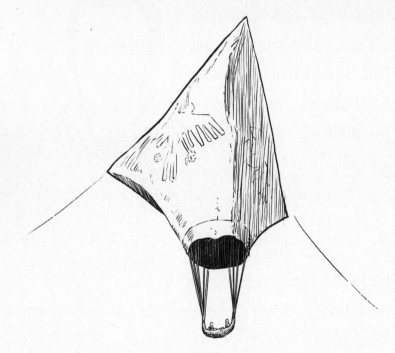

Archaeologists said there was no sign of reeds at Nazca burial sites. The reeds Woodman used were from Lake Titicaca, almost four hundred miles from the Nazca Lines. They also showed that the prevailing wind would blow balloons east into the Andes Mountains, not west over the Pacific Ocean.

It did not take long for scholars to prove that the theories of von Däniken and Woodman were false. But many people had already accepted them as true. Thousands of tourists and believers flocked to the Nazca Pampa. The sudden boom in visitors to the site put the Nazca Lines at risk.

Reiche, who had been carefully studying and protecting the lines for years, now took it upon herself to guard them. Reiche disputed the new theories, but soon her own ideas were also called into question. The Lady of the Lines believed that the Nazca Lines were a type of giant astronomical calendar. Now some scholars and scientists began to disagree with her.

CHAPTER 5
Water Lines

Since the 1940s, Maria Reiche's work had attracted interest in the Nazca Lines. It also encouraged a new generation of scientists to investigate the lines for themselves. These included an astrophysicist—a person who studies the universe and our place in it—named Gerald Hawkins in the 1960s, and an astronomer—a scientist who studies objects in the sky, including planets, stars, and galaxies—named Anthony Aveni in the 1980s.

Gerald Hawkins

Anthony Aveni

Both men wished to test Reiche's and the Kosoks' theories about the Nazca Lines being linked to the stars and acting as an astronomical calendar. What they found surprised many people, who up until then had accepted these theories as facts.

Hawkins began researching the lines in 1968. He used an early computer program to plot the lines against star constellations. He found that they did not line up with each other. He also tested the straight lines against astronomical events, such as the setting of the sun during the summer and winter solstices (the longest and shortest days of the year). He found that some lines occasionally aligned with the sun,

but the vast number did not. He did not agree
with Reiche's theories.

Hawkins's work was followed by Anthony
Aveni's in the 1980s. By both flying over the lines
and walking around them to measure their size

on the ground, Aveni made a large map of he pampa lines. He was amazed to find there were more than eight hundred! There were geometric shapes, such as triangles, rectangles, and trapezoids.

There were also zigzags, spirals, and single, double, and triple lines. Some straight lines ran for more than six miles over the pampa and up into the foothills of the Andes Mountains.

Others radiated out around a central circle, like spokes in a bicycle wheel. Aveni called these *ray centers*, as they looked like rays of light coming from the sun.

Among these lines were the animal geoglyphs, which Aveni noted seemed to have been made earlier than the straight lines and geometric shapes. A former student of his got evidence for this by dating some of the pottery pieces that had been found near the lines. Perhaps the lines and the pictures were created at different times for different reasons?

By measuring and mapping the lines, Aveni tried to match them to constellations and astronomical events, just as Hawkins had done. Aveni found that only one pattern of lines was likely to have any kind of astronomical alignment. And so Reiche's theories about the lines and constellations of stars no longer seemed believable.

Aveni thought perhaps one of the lines did align with the sun. The straight line seemed to point to the rising sun around the date of November 1. This was also the time the rainy season began high in the Andes Mountains.

The water from this rain would then make its way to the farming communities below. These communities were mainly located in the Ingenio and Nazca River valleys, on either side of the pampa.

But for Aveni, the pampa lines had a more important purpose than showing the stars or the setting sun. Instead, he thought they pointed to the places where water ran down from the Andes Mountains. Aveni believed the Nazca Lines were largely about water.

Food crops, including corn, beans, squash, potatoes, sweet potatoes, and peppers, were essential to the Nazca's survival, but they lived in one of the driest areas in the world. There were also unpredictable natural events: droughts, earthquakes, and even flash floods. Any one of these events could destroy a whole year's harvest. However, if there was no water at the start of the season, the Nazca's crops would simply not grow. Although the Nazca also fished in the Pacific Ocean, they depended on plentiful harvests to sustain them.

Inca Ceques

The Inca ceque (say: SEH-keh) system was similar to the Nazca ray center lines. However, in the ceque system, the city of Cuzco was the center of the bicycle wheel, while the ceques (the pathways) were the spokes radiating from it.

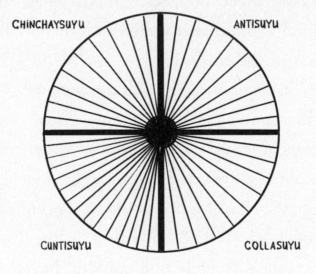

Some of the ceques paths coming out from Cuzco marked the Inca irrigation system. Other ceques marked where sacred structures were built. On another ceque line, two stone structures on a hill acted as a type of calendar. When the sun reached these structures, the Inca knew it was the right time of year to plant their crops. Some scholars believe the idea for the ceque system came from the Nazca Lines, which were made hundreds of years earlier.

To make use of all the available water, the Nazca dug out large tunnels to make underground aqueducts, today called puquíos (say: por-KEE-oss). The puquíos collected water that traveled

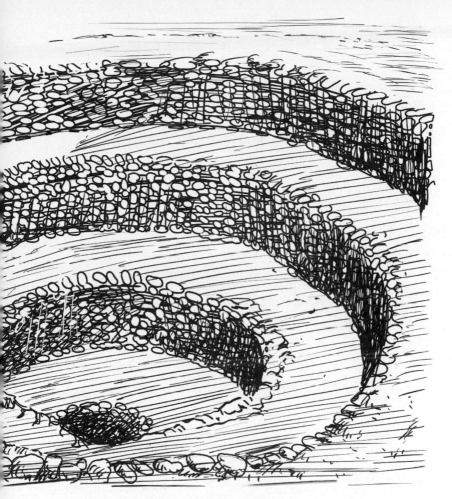

A puquío

down from the mountains and sat in underground pools and channels. The puquíos kept water moving to the Nazca's crops.

To access this water, the Nazca built funnel-shaped access holes at intervals along each puquío. Today called ojos (say: OH-hos, Spanish for *eyes*), the holes were built in spirals to make a path down to a well in the center. Here, water could be collected and the puquío accessed.

Now and then, the Nazca would climb down into the puquío to clean out debris and make sure the water kept flowing. Smaller irrigation channels would then supply the fields. As long as there wasn't a drought, water in the puquíos would keep the crops alive.

The Nazca puquíos are considered a marvel of engineering. They were so well built that some continue to irrigate fields in the region today. They proved that the Nazca understood how water traveled underground. They also showed that the Nazca had a well-developed system for large building projects. This required many people working together to achieve their goal. The same sort of cooperation was also needed to create the Nazca Lines.

It is perhaps no surprise that many scholars think the puquíos and the lines were connected. Experts estimate the puquíos were built sometime after 400 CE. This was a time of increasing

drought, which lasted centuries. Building the puquíos was one way of providing life-giving water to thirsty crops. Prayer and offerings to the Nazca gods was thought to be another.

Kon, a god of rain and wind

In the 1980s, American explorer Johan Reinhard discovered broken pottery on a sandy mountain called Cerro Blanco, which overlooks the town of Nazca. According to an ancient legend, Cerro Blanco was where a water god cried tears to help the local people overcome

a drought. Water then ran down the mountain to the dry valleys below. Reinhard thinks the pottery pieces were Nazca offerings to just such a god. His theory was that the Nazca Lines had

Johan Reinhard

nothing to do with the sky, but instead were lines pointing to where ceremonies were held to ask the gods for water. The picture geoglyphs, Reinhard said, were actually images of the mountain gods,

who the Nazca believed took the form of different animals. The geoglyphs were made big so that the gods could see them from the heavens.

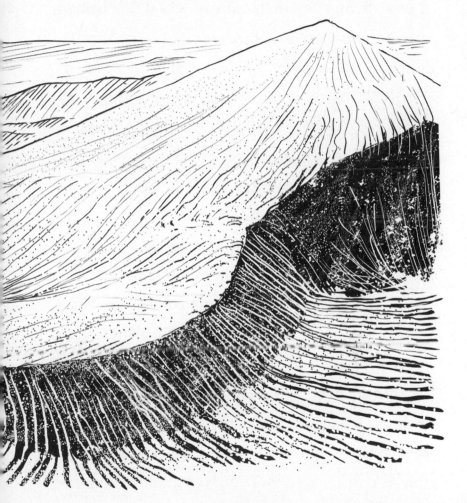

Cerro Blanco

Linking the lines with water became a popular theory. In the late 1990s, David Johnson, an American anthropologist (someone who studies human beings and their cultures), said that he had discovered more lines outside the Nazca Pampa. Some of those lines could point to sources of  water underground. Beginning in 1999, Steve Mabee, a hydrogeologist (someone who studies underground water), mapped these underground water sources. Mabee confirmed that many of the lines discovered by Johnson did in fact align with underground water—but not all of them.

Steve Mabee

By the end of the 1990s, most experts seemed to agree that the Nazca Lines were connected to locating water. Many also agreed that the lines were built to be walked around in ceremonies dedicated to the Nazca gods. What took place during these ceremonies? Perhaps the Nazca walked and danced along the lines in processions as they played musical instruments. They might have drunk from pottery vessels and then smashed them next to the lines.

Geoglyphs and Water

In northern Peru, a different set of lines have been found that archaeologists believe point to underground water sources. The lines are made up of spirals, animals, and hunting scenes, which sit between the Moche River valley and the Cerro Colorado mountain range, in an area called Quebrada de Santo Domingo. Not much is known about these lines, except for the spirals, which experts say were created by the Chimu people. The Chimu lived between 840 and 1476, nearly a thousand years after the Nazca and around 600 miles away from the Nazca Pampa. However, the position of the lines and geoglyphs near underground water channels excited archaeologists, as it seemed to strengthen the argument that the two things were connected.

It is likely that different settlements built their own picture geoglyphs. Each represented the particular god whom the people of that settlement worshipped. Aveni tried to explain: "I imagine different clans assembling in different places, walking different lines, maybe at different times; perhaps the people walked where they wished the water to flow: *Come this way.*"

In the twenty-first century, a new series of investigations into the lines began. Could they help solve the mystery of the Nazca Lines?

CHAPTER 6
The Nazca Decline

In the 2000s, new studies found there were far more Nazca Lines than anyone had previously realized. In 2006, Japanese archaeologists began a long-term investigation. Led by Masato Sakai, the team spotted many new lines using satellite imagery. Some of these lines formed birds. Then, in 2019, the team made an astonishing announcement. It had discovered over 143 new lines using a computer system equipped with artificial intelligence. The system had picked up the lines by scanning areas outside the pampa that had not been previously investigated by humans.

Most amazingly, more than forty of the newly sighted lines depicted animals, plants,

Masato Sakai

and *people*—something rarely seen before. One human figure was sixteen feet tall and six feet wide. It stood on two legs, wore a type of headdress, and appeared to be carrying a club.

In 2020, a geoglyph was found of a giant cat. Around 120 feet long, the cat was etched into the side of a hill overlooking the Nazca Pampa. It had wide eyes and seemed to be stretching out in the sun. The cat outline was beginning to suffer from erosion and parts were slipping away. More interesting was its date: the cat was thought to have been created around 200 BCE. This was too early to have been made by the Nazca.

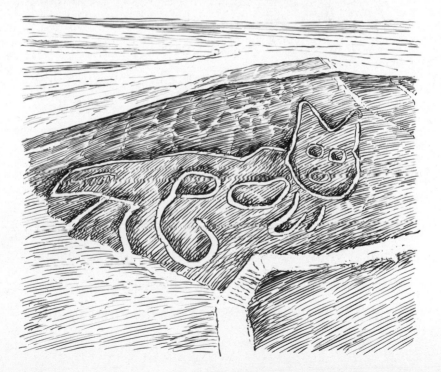

The idea of lines being created earlier than the Nazca civilization fit with studies carried out in the 2010s by a Peruvian archaeologist, Johny Isla. Using drones, Isla discovered more than a hundred new lines that predate the Nazca by hundreds of years. They were not located in the Nazca Pampa, but thirty miles north, in the Palpa Valley. The first set of lines Isla found was of a terrifying-looking creature: a killer whale with a human arm, holding a trophy head. Inside the whale's stomach were several more trophy heads. Many of the other lines in the Palpa Valley were human figures, most of which were etched into the hillside, not on the desert floor.

Johny Isla

Killer whale geoglyph

One geoglyph depicted a warrior carrying a staff and standing next to a woman. Nearby is a creature made up of a pile of snakes.

Isla thinks the Palpa figures were created by the Paracas people, who came before the Nazca. He says the figures were created between 500 and 200 BCE, during a time of great population growth. The reason the Paracas created their lines on a hillside is interesting. Perhaps this was so that people could view and appreciate them, unlike the Nazca Lines, which can only properly be seen from the air. Were the Paracas Lines made by humans for other humans to see, while the Nazca Lines were made by humans for the gods only? Isla believes that the Nazca Lines were "made with the purpose of asking the gods for water and fertility in this desert area."

The Palpa figures

It is likely the smaller Paracas lines were made by single households. But the larger Nazca Lines were made by a team of workers, perhaps even a whole village. The Palpa Valley discoveries show the lines were not made during one particular time period. Instead, line making in southern Peru seems to have been an ongoing process. The Paracas people were doing it before the Nazca arrived. Then, after the Nazca culture replaced the Paracas people, the lines—and the reasons for making them—also changed.

The Nazca occupied their territory in southern Peru for eight hundred years. Many changes occurred during that time, as is true for all civilizations. Imagine an old building in a town or city near you. Perhaps it was built as a bank over one hundred years ago. Then, for a few decades, it became a store. Now it is a café. Perhaps we can think about the Nazca Pampa in the same way. The first people living there created huge pictures of animals on the ground, a bit like the Paracas people before them. These animals represented the same gods as the Nazca depicted

on their pottery and textiles. Some were their
gods of water. They would perform ceremonies to
honor these gods, walking, dancing, singing, and
smashing pottery.

Later on, conditions on the pampa began
to change. There was a long drought and
water became a more urgent concern. To help
themselves, the Nazca built puquíos to channel
the water. They made more lines, showing where
the water was and where it came from. More

ceremonies were performed on and around these newer lines, asking the water gods for help. Many of these line images were built around Cahuachi, the Nazca's religious center. But the ceremonies were not enough to save the Nazca.

A mummified Nazca person

Sometime around 350 CE, the Nazca were hit with an earthquake and a flood that struck Cahuachi particularly hard. Buildings were destroyed and people were killed. Afterward, the center fell out of use. In a final ceremony to honor the gods, Cahuachi was buried in clay and sand. From then on, things only got worse for the Nazca.

Huarango tree

Some experts think that the Nazca helped bring about their own end by cutting down the only trees that grew in the area. A forest of huarango trees once grew in the Ica Valley, but these were cleared to grow corn and other crops. Without the trees, the earth became less fertile and there was nothing to stop the soil from being blown away by the wind. Over time, the area became even more desertlike.

Experts believe a large weather event similar to today's El Niño (a weather pattern that occurs over the Pacific Ocean) struck the Nazca lands sometime around 600 CE. This dramatic event would have brought with it terrible winds and catastrophic floods. The Nazca's remaining crops would have been torn from the ground or washed away. Without plants to keep it fertile, the soil would have dried up. Then, a long period of drought followed. For the Nazca, it may have felt like their own gods had abandoned them.

Nobody knows for sure what happened next. It is thought that the remaining Nazca people moved away from the valleys and settled at higher altitudes, above the desert region. As the Nazca had replaced the Paracas, the Nazca themselves were replaced by the Wari people, who built their capital at Cuzco. The Wari in turn were replaced by the Inca starting from around 1000 CE.

Inca woman and child

CHAPTER 7
The Nazca Lines Today

Today, the Nazca Lines are still considered one of the greatest mysteries of the ancient world. Modern scholars and scientists have been studying them for less than a century. Every year, archaeologists find new information and evidence that helps our understanding of them. And yet, the exact meaning of the Nazca Lines remains the subject of intense debate among scholars, scientists, and the public.

Tens of thousands of tourists flock to see the Nazca Lines every year. Some of these visitors still believe the lines are connected to alien life forms. There are many websites dedicated to such ideas online, even though they were shown to be false many decades ago. Although it is easy to bridge gaps in our knowledge with unproven theories, scientists continue to search for clues to establish historical facts about what occurred during the Nazca period.

Many researchers became obsessed with the Nazca Lines. Some spent decades studying them. Maria Reiche even moved to Peru permanently to dedicate her life to the lines. Her interest helped bring the lines to the public and government's attention. She convinced the Peruvian State Oil Company to build a tower on the edge of the pampa so people could climb it to see the lines from above.

Museo Maria Reiche

She also contributed to making the Nazca Pampa a UNESCO World Heritage site in 1994. An airport, a street, and a school in Nazca are named after her, and her former home near the pampa was turned into a museum. Reiche died in 1998, but while she was alive she went to great lengths to preserve the lines. She even hired three guards to stop people from straying onto the pampa and disturbing them.

However, damage to the lines caused by the public has been hard to avoid. Some people simply walk onto the pampa and step on the lines. At other times, well-meaning people damage the lines just by being careless. This happened in 2014, when Greenpeace activists protesting about climate change left footprints on a hummingbird geoglyph. In 2018, a truck driver drove onto the pampa and across three of the geoglyphs. He was arrested for destroying parts of the lines. However, Johny Isla, who is today chief archaeologist in charge of the lines, said the damage was "reparable."

While human behavior can be controlled to a point, the weather cannot. In 1998, an El Niño storm caused a mudslide that damaged some of the lines. Then, in 2009, rarely experienced rains damaged parts of another geoglyph. The rains may be a symptom of climate change—long-term shifts in temperature and weather patterns. Perhaps the same changes in climate that brought about an end to the Nazca culture will one day also destroy their legacy on the ground.

There is still plenty of time to see the Nazca Lines. Today, tourists visiting Peru can take a flight high above the lines. You can even tour them from the comfort of your home. Try zooming over them on Google Earth. Who knows? Perhaps, as recent archaeological studies have revealed, you will see something new that helps solve the ongoing riddle of the Nazca Lines.

Timeline of the Nazca Lines

c. 200 BCE	The Nazca culture replaces the Paracas culture in southern Peru
200 BCE—600 CE	The Nazca Lines are created on the Nazca Pampa
c. 350 CE	The Nazca religious center of Cahuachi is struck by an earthquake and flood
c. 400	A long period of drought begins around the Nazca Pampa, leading to the building of puquíos
c. 600	The Nazca culture is replaced by the Chavin culture
c. 1000	The Inca become the dominant people of Peru
1532	The Inca Empire is overthrown by Spanish conquistadors led by Francisco Pizarro
1926	Peruvian archaeologist Toribio Mejía Xesspe finds lines etched onto the Nazca Pampa while out hiking
1941	Paul and Rose Kosok begin studying the lines with Maria Reiche
1968	Erich von Däniken publishes *Chariots of the Gods?*, which links extraterrestrials to the Nazca Lines
1980s	Astronomer Anthony Aveni debunks Maria Reiche's theory linking the Nazca Lines to star constellations
1994	The Nazca Lines become a UNESCO World Heritage site
2019	Archaeologists discover 143 new geoglyphs

Timeline of the World

200 BCE — The Roman Republic declares on war on Macedonia, resulting in Rome's conquest of the eastern Mediterranean region

350 CE — The Wei-Zhao War breaks out in northern China after Ran Min proclaims himself emperor

c. 400 — The philosopher Hypatia becomes the first female head of the leading school in Alexandria, Egypt

c. 600 — Namri Songtsen of the Yarlung Dynasty becomes the thirty-second emperor of Tibet

c. 1000 — King Olaf Tryggvason of Norway is defeated by the Scandinavian kingdoms of Denmark and Sweden in the sea battle of Svolder

1532 — Ottoman sultan Süleyman I invades Hungary

1926 — American scientist Robert Goddard launches the first liquid-fuel rocket from a farm in Massachusetts

1968 — Civil rights leader Martin Luther King Jr. is assassinated in Memphis, Tennessee

1994 — Nelson Mandela is inaugurated as South Africa's first Black president

2019 — Scientists announce the first photo of a black hole, located in the center of the galaxy Messier 87

Bibliography

*Books for young readers

Aveni, Anthony F. *Between the Lines: The Mystery of the Giant Ground Drawings of Ancient Nasca, Peru*. Austin: University of Texas Press, 2000.

Aveni, Anthony F. *Nazca: Eighth Wonder of the World?* London: British Museum Press, 2000.

Foerster, Brien. *Nazca: Decoding the Riddle of the Lines*. Scotts Valley, CA: Amazon, 2015.

Hadingham, Evan. *Lines to the Mountain Gods*. New York: Random House, 1987.

Hawkins, Gerald S. *Beyond Stonehenge*. New York: Harper and Row, 1973.

Kosok, Paul. *Life, Land and Water in Ancient Peru*. Brooklyn, NY: Long Island University Press, 1965.

Reinhard, Johan. *The Nazca Lines: A New Perspective on Their Origin and Meaning*. Lima: Editorial Los Pinos E.I.R.L. (Kindle Edition), 1996.

*Sabol, Stephanie. *Where Are the Constellations?* New York: Penguin Workshop, 2021.

Silverman, Helaine, and Donald A. Proulx. *The Nasca*. Malden, MA: Blackwell, 2002.

von Däniken, Erich. *Chariots of the Gods?* New York: Putnam, 1970.